Play Harmonica Today!

A Complete Guide
to the Basics

by Lil' Rev

RECORDING CREDITS:

Narration, Harmonica: Lil' Rev
Engineer, Guitar: Scott Finch

ISBN 978-1-4234-3089-6

HAL•LEONARD®
CORPORATION

7777 W. BLUEMOUND RD. P.O. BOX 13819 MILWAUKEE, WI 53213

In Australia Contact:
Hal Leonard Australia Pty. Ltd.
4 Lentara Court
Cheltenham, Victoria, 3192 Australia
Email: ausadmin@halleonard.com.au

Visit Hal Leonard Online at
www.halleonard.com

Introduction

Welcome to *Play Harmonica Today!*—This book is designed to get you started on this fun and exciting instrument, with everything you need to know to play melodies and chords, and to learn songs you love to play. This book is written for use with a standard, 10-hole diatonic harmonica in the key of C major.

About the CD

The accompanying CD will take you step by step through each lesson and each music example. Much like a real lesson, the best way to learn this material is to read and practice a while at first on your own, then listen to the CD. With *Play Harmonica Today!* you can learn at your own pace. If there is ever something that you don't quite understand the first time through, go back to the CD and listen to the track number listed to replay the teacher's explanation. Every musical track has been given its own track number, so if you want to practice a song again, you can find it right away.

Contents

The Basics

Congratulations! You have found your way to the noblest of little instruments—the mouth organ! You are now about to embark on a fascinating journey that will take you back almost 200 years in American history, from the Wild West and the Civil War to the Mississippi river boats and World War II. Wherever regular folks have traveled, the harmonica has accompanied them, just like it will accompany you as you begin to blow the blues or play a campfire classic.

Harmonica History

The humble harmonica's history can be traced back thousands of years to a free-reed instrument of China known as the *sheng*. It wasn't until the early 1820s, however, that German clockmakers Christen Frederick, Ludwig Buschmann, and Christian Messner developed and expanded on the ancient free-reed concept by putting pitch pipes together. Their development led to the early lead plate models with round holes and brass reeds. In the 1850s, a young Mathias Hohner of Trossingen, Germany began to mass produce harmonicas that sold like hot cakes, quickly gaining popularity in all of Europe, and then in the United States.

The harmonica's appeal hasn't changed much in that it is still both portable and affordable, making it the instrument of choice among the working folks of all lands. Furthermore, harmonica legends of the last 100 years have given us a remarkable recorded legacy that will continue to inspire us to push the limits of this tiny pocket piano for years to come.

Blues, jazz, classical, folk, bluegrass, rock 'n' roll, you name it, it's all possible! So, what are you waiting for? Let's jump right in and begin with some of the most basic elements of playing, learning how to hold the harmonica, lip position, and learning how to play one note at a time.

Care for Your Harmonica

Most harmonicas could potentially last a lifetime. What determines whether or not your harmonica will be a family heirloom is how much you use it and how well you take care of it. Below is a list of important dos and don'ts that every beginner should be aware of as he or she is starting out.

- **Always keep your harmonica in its case.** Carrying it in your pocket or backpack without the case will allow dust, dirt, and lint to clog up the reeds. If you lose your case, a Ziploc baggy will do.

- **Never allow others to play your harmonica.** You're liable to spread germs.

- **You don't have to blow the harmonica really hard in order to produce a sound.** Start out blowing gently until you get used to how it responds.

- **Never eat or drink anything and then play the harmonica without first rinsing out your mouth.** Food particles and sugary drinks will get in your harmonica and clog up the reeds. Simply swish a little water around in your mouth before you play.

- **Tap your harmonica out on your leg before putting it away.** This will clear it of any excess moisture.

- **Be careful with young kids around.** Avoid putting the harmonica in their mouths or blowing it too close to their ears. Choking or hurting ear drums is possible.

Holding the Harmonica

Learning to hold the harmonica properly is the harmonica player's first priority. Here are a couple of important rules of thumb:

1. **Numbers Up**: The numbers 1–10 should always be right side up and facing you with the lowest numbers on the left-hand side.

2. **Left Hand**: While you may find a few who do it differently, 99 percent of the time the harmonica is held in the left hand. The right hand is used to control tremolo, vibrato, and cupping effects (more on those later).

Lip Position

Sounding one note at a time is every harmonica player's second priority. Once you can play a single note, then you are on your way to playing an actual melody.

To start, we'll focus on what is generally referred to as *lipping*, or pursing your lips. This is the easiest way to play a single note. Imagine drinking soda through a straw. This is exactly how your lips should be shaped. Notice the image below. See how the circle surrounds just one hole at a time? This is your goal.

► If you are having trouble, say the word "you" slowly and your lips will form perfectly in the soda-through-the-straw shape.

Reading Harmonica Music

► In the few instances where you may not recognize the song or its melody, spend some time listening to the accompanying CD.

There are two ways to read harmonica music. The first is called **standard music notation**. While this system requires time to learn, once mastered, it allows you to literally play any piece of music you want. This book will provide you with the necessary rudimentary knowledge of standard music notation to learn to play the harmonica.

The second way is known as the **number/arrow system** and is extremely easy to learn. The numbers relate to the numbered holes on your harmonica and the arrows designate up (↑) for **blow** (blowing out) or down (↓) for **draw** (drawing in). While this system is not as precise as standard music notation, it's much easier to learn. And, since our objective is to get you playing harmonica quickly, this book will rely primarily on the number/arrow system.

Okay! Let's get started. Here is what you need to know in order to play the harmonica using either the number/arrow or the standard notation system:

Notes

A musical **note** will indicate two things:

1. **Pitch**: How high or low the sound is that the note represents.
2. **Rhythmic Value**: How many beats the note is held or played.

Here are four kinds of notes:

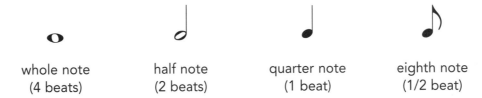

| whole note | half note | quarter note | eighth note |
| (4 beats) | (2 beats) | (1 beat) | (1/2 beat) |

Therefore, it follows that:

- ■ Two half notes equal one whole note.
- ■ Two quarter notes equal one half note.
- ■ Four quarter notes equal one whole note.

Staff

A musical **staff** has five lines and four spaces. Each line and each space represents a different pitch.

Clef

Harmonica music is written with a treble clef that looks like this:

The **treble clef** indicates the names of the lines and spaces by showing you where G is located, and for that reason it is also known as a G clef. Notice how the bottom of the clef curls around the second line. That line is the note G. The names of the lines and spaces are in alphabetical order going up so the next space is A, the following line B, and so on.

► One easy way to remember the notes for the lines is to say "Every Good Boy Does Fine." The notes for the spaces spell the word "FACE."

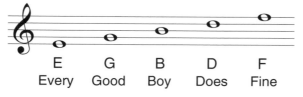

E — Every
G — Good
B — Boy
D — Does
F — Fine

F   A   C   E
"FACE"

Measures

Notes on a staff are divided into **measures**. Measures help keep things organized so you know where you are while playing or singing a song.

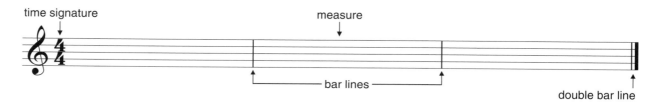

time signature

measure

bar lines

double bar line

Time Signature

A **time signature** determines how many beats will appear in each measure. There are two numbers and they are important. The top number tells you how many beats will be in each measure, and the bottom number will tell you what type of note will equal one beat.

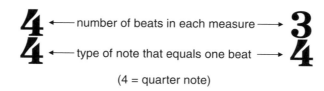

4 ← number of beats in each measure → 3
4 ← type of note that equals one beat → 4

(4 = quarter note)

Number/Arrow System

Reading harmonica music with the number/arrow system is, as I mentioned earlier, very easy. If an arrow is pointing up (↑), it means to blow out. If an arrow is pointing down (↓), it means to draw in or inhale. First you look at the number and find it on the harp. Then you look at the arrow and either blow or draw. It's that simple. The downside is that, unlike the standard notation system, there is no indication of how long to hold a note. So, the number/arrow system is best used on old favorites and melodies that you already know. If you come across one you don't know in this book, listen to the CD a couple times to get the idea.

Remember: ↑ = blow   ↓ = draw

Track 1

First Exercises

- Before we can begin playing the first position major scale, let's get acquainted with the full range of the harmonica.

- Locate hole #1 on your harmonica and blow out (↑) on hole #1. Listen to how low this note sounds. It's called low C.

- Now, draw (↓) on hole #1. This is called low D. It is also a very low sounding note.

- Find hole #4. It's located right in the middle of the harmonica. Good! Now, blow out on hole #4↑. This is called C and it has a midrange pitch.

- As you guessed it, draw on hole #4↓. This is also a midrange note called D.

- Well, we're almost there. Try this same pattern of blowing and drawing on holes #7 and #10. When you blow on holes #7 and #10, you are also playing the note C in the upper range of the harmonica.

7↑   7↓   10↑   10↓

To really hear the full range of the harmonica, put the harmonica up to your mouth at hole #1 and slowly blow out while sliding up to hole #10. Can you hear the sound go from low to high? Now, breathe in (draw) on hole #1 and slide up to hole #10. Can you hear the whole range of draw notes from low to high?

Here's a handy chart of all the notes on the harmonica:

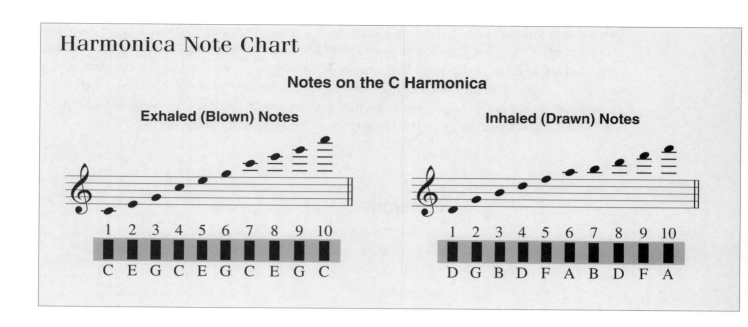

Track 2

The C Major Scale

The **C major scale** (C–D–E–F–G–A–B–C, or do–re–mi–fa–sol–la–ti–do) is the foundation on which all of our single note studies will rest. By learning to play the C major scale, we are accomplishing three things. We are:

1. Learning to play individual notes clearly and smoothly.

2. Learning the names of the notes and their placement on the staff.

3. Learning to play by ear (listening).

To begin, we will simply focus on the numbers and the direction of our breath. Let's go up the scale first with this exercise.

4↑   4↓   5↑   5↓   6↑   6↓   7↓   7↑

Great! Now let's go down the scale.

7↑ 7↓ 6↓ 6↑ 5↓ 5↑ 4↓ 4↑

Ok, now up and down again.

4↑ 4↓ 5↑ 5↓ 6↑ 6↓ 7↓ 7↑
7↑ 7↓ 6↓ 6↑ 5↓ 5↑ 4↓ 4↑

Great! Now, try to play the scale a couple of times without looking at the numbers and arrows.

Excellent! Now, perform the scale ascending one last time playing each note twice.

4↑ 4↑ 4↓ 4↓ 5↑ 5↑ 5↓ 5↓
6↑ 6↑ 6↓ 6↓ 7↓ 7↓ 7↑ 7↑

Articulation

Playing repeated notes points out another basic technique we must learn: *articulation* or *tonguing*. Articulation is the way we begin a sound on an instrument. Instead of just blowing, say "ta" to start the air stream. Don't use your voice, but mouth the syllable "ta" to begin every note or chord (more on chords later). When tonguing drawn notes, many players simply draw and allow the change in direction of the air to create a clean start to the note, while others use a word like "ta." Later in this book, other words will be suggested for you to "say" to achieve different sounds or styles on the harmonica. Experiment with this to create other methods of expressing your music through the way you articulate.

Now, repeat the lesson on the C major scale using "ta" or tonguing each note.

Our First Songs

► Please listen to the CD if you don't know some of these classics.

Here are some basic melodies that you probably already know. By starting with simple folk songs, we can hear if we are playing them right or wrong.

Track 3

Mary Had a Little Lamb

5↑ 4↓ 4↑ 4↓   5↑ 5↑ 5↑   4↓ 4↓ 4↓   5↑ 6↑ 6↑
5↑ 4↓ 4↑ 4↓   5↑ 5↑ 5↑   4↓ 4↓   5↑ 4↓ 4↑

Track 4

Skip to My Lou

5↑ 4↑   5↑ 5↑ 5↑ 6↑   4↓ 3↓   4↓ 4↓ 4↓ 5↓
5↑ 4↑   5↑ 5↑ 5↑ 6↑   4↓ 5↑ 5↓ 5↑ 4↓ 4↑ 4↑

Track 5

The Farmer in the Dell

3↑ 4↑ 4↑ 4↑ 4↑ 4↑   4↓ 5↑ 5↑ 5↑ 5↑ 5↑
6↑ 6↑ 6↓ 6↑ 5↑ 4↑   4↓ 5↑ 5↑ 4↓ 4↓ 4↑

Track 6

(Oh, My Darling) Clementine

4↑ 4↑ 4↑ 3↑   5↑ 5↑ 5↑ 4↑   4↑ 5↑ 6↑ 6↑ 5↓ 5↑ 4↓
4↓ 5↑ 5↓ 5↓   5↑ 4↓ 5↑ 4↑   4↑ 5↑ 4↓ 3↓ 3↓ 4↓ 4↑

Track 7

When the Saints Go Marching In

4↑ 5↑ 5↓ 6↑   4↑ 5↑ 5↓ 6↑
4↑ 5↑ 5↓ 6↑ 5↑ 4↑ 5↑ 4↓

5↑ 5↑ 4↓ 4↑ 4↑   5↑ 6↑ 6↑ 5↓ 5↑
5↓ 6↑ 5↑ 4↑ 4↓ 4↑

More Easy Favorites

Here are three more old-time favorites. Your goal is to learn how to play one note at a time.

Track 8

Oh! Susanna

► Reminder: shape your lips like you're sipping soda through a straw.

4↑ 4↓ 5↑ 6↑ 6↑ 6↓ 6↑ 5↑ 4↑ 4↓ 5↑ 5↑ 4↓ 4↑ 4↓

4↑ 4↓ 5↑ 6↑ 6↑ 6↓ 6↑ 5↑ 4↑ 4↓ 5↑ 5↑ 4↓ 4↓ 4↑

5↓ 5↓ 6↓ 6↓ 6↓ 6↑ 6↑ 5↑ 4↑ 4↓

4↑ 4↓ 5↑ 6↑ 6↑ 6↓ 6↑ 5↑ 4↑ 4↓ 5↑ 5↑ 4↓ 4↓ 4↑

Track 9

Camptown Races

6↑ 6↑ 5↑ 6↑ 6↓ 6↑ 5↑   5↑ 4↓   5↑ 4↓

6↑ 6↑ 5↑ 6↑ 6↓ 6↑ 5↑   4↓ 5↓ 5↑ 4↓ 4↑

4↑ 4↑ 5↑ 6↑ 7↑   6↓ 6↓ 7↑ 6↓ 6↑

5↑ 5↓ 6↑ 6↑ 5↑ 6↑ 6↓ 6↑ 5↑ 4↓ 5↑ 5↓ 5↑ 4↓ 4↑

Here's a good introduction to playing songs in the upper register of your harmonica.

Track 10

Tom Dooley

6↑ 6↑ 6↑ 6↓ 7↑ 8↑ 8↑   6↑ 6↑ 6↑ 6↓ 7↑ 8↓

6↑ 6↑ 6↑ 6↓ 7↑ 8↓ 8↓   8↓ 8↓ 8↑ 7↑ 6↓ 7↑

More on Reading Music

While a great deal of the notation in this book will focus on the number/arrow system, you may also want to memorize the notes in standard notation with their corresponding blow or draw positions.

Octaves

This is a good time to learn the word **octave**. An octave is the interval of eight scale degrees between two notes of the same name. Look at the C major scale below. It begins on C and ends on C. Those Cs are one octave apart.

Most of the standard notation in this book is written one octave lower than the harmonica sounds. This was done to keep the notes on the staff so they are easier to read (instead of above the staff).

C Major Scale

Once you have memorized this you will be able to play almost any basic melody written in standard notation. Eventually you will be playing higher and lower notes, above and below the staff.

Try thinking the name of each note as you play it in the following exercise:

Rests

Rests are measured silent spaces used in music. The following rests will appear throughout this book:

Think of a rest as a pause of a definite length, or an opportunity to... rest!

Dotted Notes

Dotted notes are a way that we can extend the value of a note. A dot extends a note by one half of its original value. For example: A half note ♩ (two beats) plus a dot "·" (one beat) = a dotted half note ♩· (three beats). The five measures below show different ways to fill a measure with four beats in 4/4 time:

Pickup Notes

Sometimes a song begins with an incomplete measure with what are called **pickup notes** (sometimes there's only one). The pickup measure will contain fewer beats than are called for in the time signature. No cause for concern, but worth mentioning as some of you will notice something wrong with the first measure of the next four songs in this book. Check out this example using pickup notes:

Ties

A *tie* connects two notes to create one long note. The second note is not tongued or restarted and its value is added to the first note. Keep drawing or blowing until the value of the tied note is complete. In the example below, the value of the first tie is three beats because a half note (two beats) and a quarter note (one beat) are combined to equal three beats. What is the value of the second tie? Right! It's four beats because the tie combines the value of two half notes which are two beats each.

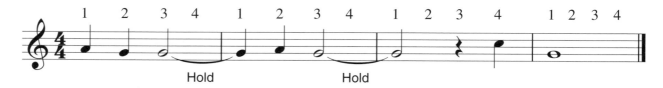

Here's one from New Orleans that everyone ought to know. Remember to hold a whole note (four beats) tied to a quarter note (one beat) for five total beats. This time there's standard notation, pickup notes, plus the CD has a guitar accompaniment!

Track 11

When the Saints Go Marching In #2

Track 12

How Dry I Am!

► Pay attention to the whole notes with the ties.

Try this cowboy classic. You'll find quarter notes, half notes, whole notes, and dotted half notes.

Track 13

The Red River Valley

► Remember to listen to the CD to get a feel for the melody.

Track 14

Wildwood Flower

The Upper Register

Track 15

Once you have mastered the C major scale in the middle register (from the last lesson), it is time to start moving up to the next octave. Let's review by playing "Taps" in the low/middle register. Then we'll try it in the upper register.

Taps

3↑ 3↑ 4↑   3↑ 4↑ 5↑   3↑ 4↑ 5↑   3↑ 4↑ 5↑

3↑ 4↑ 5↑   4↑ 5↑ 6↑   5↑ 4↑ 3↑   3↑ 3↑ 4↑

Good! Now let's try it an octave higher.

► Note that because the reeds are smaller and stiffer in the upper octave, the amount of air it takes to produce pitch will vary by a small degree.

Taps #2

6↑ 6↑ 7↑   6↑ 7↑ 8↑   6↑ 7↑ 8↑   6↑ 7↑ 8↑

6↑ 7↑ 8↑   7↑ 8↑ 9↑   8↑ 7↑ 6↑   6↑ 6↑ 7↑

Very good! Now you are ready for this upper register exercise.

6↑ 6↑ 7↑ 8↓ 9↑   6↑ 6↑ 7↑ 8↓ 9↑

8↑ 8↑ 8↓ 7↓ 7↑   8↑ 8↑ 8↓ 7↓ 7↑   6↑ 7↑

First we'll explore this simple bluegrass melody in the middle register. Then we'll follow with the same melody in the higher register.

Track 16

Boil Them Cabbage Down #1

Now we'll follow with the same melody in the higher register. Remember, the high end does not require as much air to produce a pitch. So blow gently.

Track 17

Boil Them Cabbage Down #2

Repeat Signs and Endings

Repeat signs are double bar lines with two dots, as shown in measures 1, 8, 10, and 17 of the song "Oh, Them Golden Slippers." Just as the name implies, repeat signs tell you to play certain passages twice. The brackets above measures 8 and 9 indicate first and second *endings* to the repeated section.

Here's what you do:

- Play the first line up to the repeat sign at the end of measure 8 (the first ending).

- Without missing a beat, go back to the first repeat sign at the beginning of measure 1.

- Play the first seven measures, skip measure 8, and play measure 9 instead (next page).

- Keep going to the next line and play to measure 17. Repeat to measure 10 and the song ends at measure 17 the second time.

First listen to the recording a few times and then begin to follow the notation or numbers and arrows.

Oh, Them Golden Slippers

▶ Remember to tap a steady beat with your foot; count 1-2-3-4.

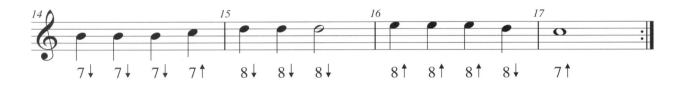

Notes Above 7th Hole C

For those of you following standard notation, notice that it is common for the notes to rise above 7th hole C on the staff. Take a few moments to memorize each note's placement on the staff, as well as its corresponding number and arrow.

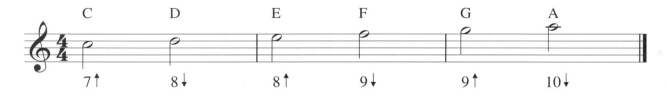

Slur

A *slur* is similar to a tie. A tie connects notes that are the same and combines their values without tonguing the tied note. A slur connects notes that are different, but similarly, the connected note is not tongued. You might've noticed some slurs being played in the previous song "Oh, Them Golden Slippers." Here are some examples:

This well-known Irish classic will get you playing on both the high and low end of the harmonica, making it a great piece to master.

Track 19

Danny Boy

The Train Sound

Track 20

The *train sound* is synonymous with the old-time harmonica repertoire. This simple exercise will get you moving in the right direction with a basic chugging pattern.

Chords

To create the train sound, you are not going to be playing single notes. Instead, you'll be playing groups of notes together. These groups are known as *chords*. So, when you see the numbers "432" or "321" written together vertically with one arrow next to them, this means that you will be playing all three notes together at one time, as a chord. For more on playing chords, see Lesson 7.

Start slowly and gradually pick up speed as you go. Imagine the sound of a train pulling out of the station. It starts slowly and then gradually gets faster.

Train Pattern

```
4|  4|  4↑  4↑  3|  3|  3↑  3↑  4|  4|  4↑  4↑  3|  3|  3↑  3↑
3|  3|  3|  3|  2|  2|  2|  2|  3|  3|  3|  3|  2|  2|  2|  2|
2↓  2↓  2|  2|  1↓  1↓  1|  1|  2↓  2↓  2|  2|  1↓  1↓  1|  1|
```

Repeat the pattern above as many times as possible. When you can keep a steady beat going, then you are ready to add the *whistle*.

To blow the whistle, breathe in (draw) on holes 3 and 4 together while trying to shape the sound "wah wah" with your mouth each time. Try to hold the second 3 and 4 a little longer than the first one.

Track 21

Whistle Pattern

```
4|        4|
3↓        3↓
WAH       WAAH
```

Music History

Fantastic train pieces have been recorded by Big Water Horton, Freeman Stowers, Deford Bailey, and Sonny Terry. Be sure to seek them out!

Lesson 6 Playing in 3/4 Time

When a song is played in 3/4 time, we count 1-2-3, 1-2-3, or oom-pah-pah, oom-pah-pah. It is notated like this:

► In the 3/4 time signature, the number 3 on the top indicates that there are three beats to a measure. The number 4 on the bottom means a quarter note is equal to one beat.

Some classic songs in 3/4 time include, "Goodnight Irene," "The Tennessee Waltz," "On Top of Old Smokey," Down in the Valley," and "Streets of Laredo."

When Irish Eyes Are Smiling

In this song there are dotted notes, but these are dotted quarter notes. Remember a dot extends the note by half of its value. Therefore a quarter note (one beat) and a dot (one half beat) equals one and a half beats. On the CD, the song starts with a short guitar introduction.

Ach Du Lieber Augustin (O My Dearest Augustine)

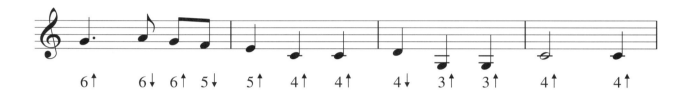

Music History

"Ach Du Lieber Augustin (O My Dearest Augustine)" originated in Vienna during the plague period of 1768–1769. Legend has it that one evening, Augustine hoisted one too many glasses of wine and decided on a nap halfway home. The morning corpse patrol threw his body on the cart with the other corpses and took him away. Fortunately, Augustine awoke in the nick of time, to the horror of the mortician. In no time at all, the rumor spread far and wide that wine was not only a cure, but also a great deterrent for the plague.

"A Bicycle Built for Two (Daisy Bell)" is a lovely sentimental song that makes great practice for playing in 3/4 time with lots of dotted half notes and ties. Be sure to try it with a very slow, lilting feel.

A Bicycle Built for Two (Daisy Bell)

Track 24

► Remember, in 3/4 time we count 1-2-3, 1-2-3, and the dot on a note extends it by half of its value. So a dotted half note equals three beats.

More practice in 3/4 time. Count 1-2-3, 1-2-3, 1-2-3. Remember this symbol is called a tie. A tie connects two notes together and the value of the second note is added to the first.

My Bonnie Lies Over the Ocean

Track 25

23

The national anthem of baseball sounds great on the harmonica. Play it in turtle style… slowly. Remember this symbol 𝄽 is called a quarter rest. Its value is equal to one beat. The harmonica begins after a short guitar intro on the CD.

Take Me Out to the Ball Game

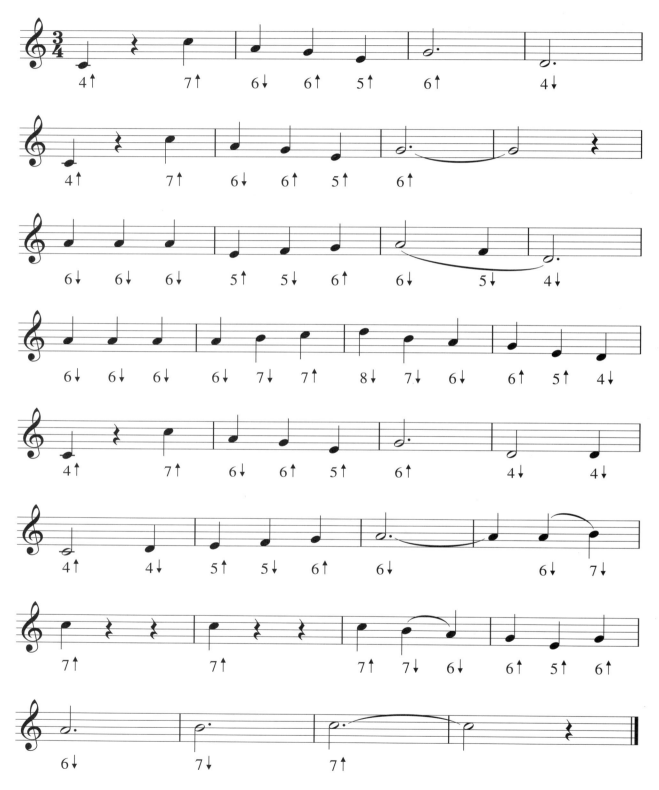

Now you should have a good feel for playing melodies in 3/4 time or oom-pah-pah time!

Play this next song slowly and mournfully. It is a cowboy classic and well suited for those camp-fire sing-a-longs we all enjoy so much. Count: 1-2-3, 1-2-3, 1-2-3.

Home on the Range

Playing Rhythm

Track 28

Thus far, we have focused primarily on playing individual notes, or the melody on the harmonica. Now it's time to explore the art of playing rhythm or accompaniment style. To play rhythm on the harmonica, we'll have to play several notes at once. These groups of notes are called *chords*. When we play single notes, we're puckering our lips like drinking through a straw. To play chords, we'll need to open our mouths a little wider in order to play multiple notes at once.

Once you learn to play some basic chordal accompaniment patterns, it becomes much easier to make music with others. Let's play our first chord—the G chord. We'll play four four-chord groups in this exercise.

► Remember, ↓ means to draw and ↑ means to blow.

Count:	1	2	3	4	1	2	3	4	1	2	3	4	1	2	3	4
G Chord	3 2 1↓	3 2 1↓	3 2 1↓	3 2 1↓	3 2 1↓	3 2 1↓	3 2 1↓	3 2 1↓	3 2 1↓	3 2 1↓	3 2 1↓	3 2 1↓	3 2 1↓	3 2 1↓	3 2 1↓	3 2 1↓

Good! Now, let's try the second chord, which is a C chord.

Count:	1	2	3	4	1	2	3	4	1	2	3	4	1	2	3	4
C Chord	6↑ 5 4	6↑ 5 4	6↑ 5 4	6↑ 5 4	6↑ 5 4	6↑ 5 4	6↑ 5 4	6↑ 5 4	6↑ 5 4	6↑ 5 4	6↑ 5 4	6↑ 5 4	6↑ 5 4	6↑ 5 4	6↑ 5 4	6↑ 5 4

Next we'll play our third chord, which is called a D chord.

Count:	1	2	3	4	1	2	3	4	1	2	3	4	1	2	3	4
D Chord	5 4↓	5 4↓	5 4↓	5 4↓	5 4↓	5 4↓	5 4↓	5 4↓	5 4↓	5 4↓	5 4↓	5 4↓	5 4↓	5 4↓	5 4↓	5 4↓

This one is a variation on the train pattern you learned earlier.

Blues Train

Count:	1	2	3	4	1	2	3	4	1	2	3	4	1	2	3	4
	4	4	3↑	3↑	3↑	3↑	4	4	3	3	3↑	3↑	3↑	3↑	4	4
	3	3	2	2	2	2	3	3	2	2	2	2	2	2	3	3
	2↓	2↓	1	1	1	1	2↓	2↓	1↓	1↓	1	1	1	1	2↓	2↓

1	2	3	4	1	2	3	4
3	3	3↑	3↑	3↑	3↑	4	4
2	2	2	2	2	2	3	3
1↓	1↓	1	1	1	1	2↓	2↓

Excellent! Now let's put all of this together in a basic 12-bar blues pattern.

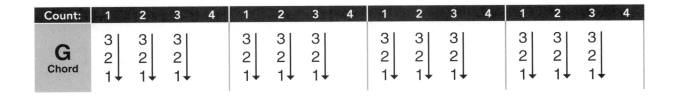

Count:	1	2	3	4	1	2	3	4	1	2	3	4	1	2	3	4
G Chord	3 2 1↓	3 2 1↓	3 2 1↓		3 2 1↓	3 2 1↓	3 2 1↓		3 2 1↓	3 2 1↓	3 2 1↓		3 2 1↓	3 2 1↓	3 2 1↓	

	1	2	3	4	1	2	3	4	1	2	3	4	1	2	3	4
C Chord	6↑ 5 4	6↑ 5 4	6↑ 5 4		6↑ 5 4	6↑ 5 4	6↑ 5 4	**G** Chord	3 2 1↓	3 2 1↓	3 2 1↓		3 2 1↓	3 2 1↓	3 2 1↓	

	1	2	3	4	1	2	3	4	1	2	3	4	1	2	3	4
D Chord	5 4↓	5 4↓	5 4↓	**C** Chord	6↑ 5 4	6↑ 5 4	6↑ 5 4	**G** Chord	3 2 1↓	3 2 1↓	3 2 1↓		3 2 1↓	3 2 1↓	3 2 1↓	

One of the great rhythm harp pieces of all time is called "Room to Move" by John Mayall. While it borrowed heavily from the classic Sonny Boy Williamson song "One Way Out," Mayall's rendition became a standard. Here's a generic version of this pattern.

Let's finish with the Bo Diddley beat. This is a signature rock 'n' roll riff that makes for great practice on the G chord.

► This riff has a tricky rhythm, so please listen to the CD a couple times to get the feel.

play these two fast

Lesson 8 | Soaking Your Harmonica?

Some blues players believed that soaking their traditional wood-model harmonicas in water would make them more airtight. Models such as Hohner's Marine Band or Blues Harp models have wooden combs that often swell due to moisture, and the idea that putting them in water might help them has never made sense to this author!

First of all, the excess moisture can and will create corrosion on some of the inner parts if it is not tapped out enough. Secondly, the company does not encourage it, nor do they recommend it in their warranty. Also, if your harmonica is a wood-combed instrument, the excess water can make the paint crack and peel, as well as the wood's outer surface. Lastly, if the wood swells too much it can injure your lips and your harmonica will require filing on the swollen surfaces. Filing surfaces on your harmonica can cause it to plug up.

Harmonica Tidbits

Here are a few cool harmonica tidbits:

- It was said that Frank and Jesse James were harmonica players and that a harmonica in Frank's shirt pocket once saved his life by stopping a bullet!

- The harmonica was played by Honest Abe at the Lincoln-Douglas debates.

- The harmonica was the first instrument in outer space, when it was smuggled onboard one of the early Gemini space flights.

- In 1896 the harmonica sold for a mere fifty cents!

- The late, great Lonnie Glosson could make his harmonica talk saying, "I want my momma," or, "I want a little drink of water."

- Many of today's greatest pop stars play the mouth organ including Billy Joel, Bruce Springsteen, Mick Jagger, Bob Dylan, Neil Young, and John Lennon.

- President Warren G. Harding kept a collection of harmonicas while he was in the White House.

Track 33

Lesson 9 Playing Tremolo

Tremolo (also known as ***vibrato***) is a beautiful, wavering sound that can be produced on almost every instrument, but is particularly pleasing when played on the harmonica. It's often referred to as that "campfire sound."

Tremolo is created when the right hand oscillates back and forth directly in front of the harmonica, creating a shaking sound.

Here's how it's done:

1. Hold your harmonica in your left hand.

2. Place your right hand around the front of the harmonica with your right thumb resting just under the bottom right end of the harp.

3. Blow or draw on any hole.

4. Move your right hand back and forth in front of the harmonica in a fanning motion towards the front of the harmonica.

As you move your right hand back and forth in front of the harmonica, you'll hear the pitch change as it becomes wavy. A great way to practice this is to start out by playing the C major scale once through and then play it with tremolo.

4↑ 4↓ 5↑ 5↓ 6↑ 6↓ 7↓ 7↑   7↑ 7↓ 6↓ 6↑ 5↓ 5↑ 4↓ 4↑

Now play it up and down without stopping.

4↑ 4↓ 5↑ 5↓ 6↑ 6↓ 7↓ 7↑ 7↑ 7↓ 6↓ 6↑ 5↓ 5↑ 4↓ 4↑

Lastly, let's mix it up a bit and go all the way to the 10 hole and back.

4↑ 4↓ 5↑ 5↓ 6↑ 6↓ 7↓ 7↑ 8↓ 8↑ 9↓ 9↑ 10↓

9↑ 9↓ 8↑ 8↓ 7↑ 7↓ 6↓ 6↑ 5↓ 5↑ 4↓ 4↑

Music History

Two fine examples of great tremolo playing are country-western harmonica whiz Charlie McCoy and blues legend Sonny Boy Williamson.

Track 34

Two Great Songs for Playing Tremolo

Let's concentrate exclusively on playing tremolo. Following the number/arrow system will make it easier. If you do not know the melody, listen to the CD once or twice.

As you practice these two pieces, listen for the spaces where there would be whole notes or half notes (if these were written in standard notation). These notes are held longer and are perfect places to use your right-hand tremolo technique.

Kum Ba Yah

4↑ 5↑ 6↑ 6↑ 6↑ 6↓ 6↓ 6↑

4↑ 5↑ 6↑ 6↑ 6↑ 5↓ 5↑ 4↓

4↑ 5↑ 6↑ 6↑ 6↑ 6↓ 6↓ 6↑

5↓ 5↑ 4↑ 4↓ 4↓ 4↑

Michael Row Your Boat Ashore

4↑ 5↑ 6↑ 5↑ 6↑ 6↓ 6↑

5↑ 6↑ 6↓   6↑

5↑ 6↑ 6↑ 5↑ 5↓ 5↑ 4↓

4↑ 4↓ 5↑ 4↓ 4↑

Holiday Songs

Now let's add a few holiday songs to our repertoire. Try adding tremolo to some of these songs. Note that "Jingle Bells" starts with four measures of guitar before the harmonica part comes in.

Jingle Bells

This is an exceptionally pretty piece when played with tremolo.

Silent Night

Track 37

We Wish You a Merry Christmas

Try this using tremolo. It is beautiful.

Track 38

O Come, All Ye Faithful
(Adeste Fideles)

Cross Harp and Bending

Professional harmonica players will use as many as twelve different positions when playing a 10-hole harmonica, like the one you are using. For our purposes, we will only describe and demonstrate four of those positions. These four positions are briefly defined below. Some of the positions, because of their more complicated nature, will be explained further in the following pages.

Understanding Position Playing

First Position (straight harp or major): In first position you are playing the harmonica in the key to which it is tuned. This means that if you start by blowing on the 4th hole and continue as indicated below, you will be playing a major scale in the key of your harmonica, in this case, the key of C.

	C	D	E	F	G	A	B	C
	4↑	4↓	5↑	5↓	6↑	6↓	7↓	7↑

This scale can also be played an octave higher and an octave lower on your harmonica, but you will need to learn how to bend notes before you can gain that flexibility... more on bending notes later. Good examples of first position songs include, "Home on the Range," "Oh! Susanna," "Turkey in the Straw," "This Land Is Your Land," and thousands more, including most of the songs in this book.

Second Position (*Cross Harp*): Second position is commonly known as **cross harp** and begins with a draw on the 2nd hole and continues as indicated below. This is known as a simplified blues scale in G. Note that the B♭ and the D♭ have a different arrow for indicating the draw. These arrows mean you are to bend the note. After a brief introduction of third and fourth positions below, we will learn how to bend notes.

	G	B♭	C	D♭	D	F	G
	2↓	3↘	4↑	4↘	4↓	5↓	6↑

Good examples of second position classics include "Whammer Jammer," "Juke," "Low Rider," "Honky Tonk Women," and "When the Levee Breaks."

Third Position (minor): Third position is used for playing in a minor key. Begin with D (played by a draw on the 4th hole) and continue as indicated below. This is actually a scale in the Dorian mode which gives a minor feel. *Modes* are types of scales.

D	E	F	G	A	B	C	D
4↓	5↑	5↓	6↑	6↓	7↓	7↑	8↓

Fourth Position (minor): Fourth position is also used for playing in a minor key. Begin with A, played by a draw on the 6th hole, and continue as indicated below. This is an A minor scale.

A	B	C	D	E	F	G	A
6↓	7↓	7↑	8↓	8↑	9↓	9↑	10↓

Good examples of fourth position songs include "House of the Rising Sun," "Summertime," "Ain't No Sunshine," and "Saint James Infirmary."

Track 39

Bending

Cross harp, otherwise known as second position, simply means that you are playing your C harmonica in the key of G. Some of the notes in the scale will have to be lowered or **bent** to create the blues scale. Because note-bending is not only used for cross harp, we will spend some time learning how to bend notes on the harmonica.

Thus far you have used the C major scale as your home base. Now you will begin to use the G simplified blues scale, which can be found on your C harmonica by starting on the 2nd hole draw. Once again, here is how the complete scale looks with the bends.

G	B♭	C	D♭	D	F	G
2↓	3↘	4↑	4↘	4↓	5↓	6↑

Learning to bend notes to lower their pitch will take a little practice, but with persistence it will come. Let's get started and find out just how it is done.

Track 40

Getting Started:

1. Drawing in on the 1st hole, say the words "wee-ooo." These syllables will help put your lips and mouth in the right position to bend a note. Try it again; can you hear the pitch change as you draw in and say "wee-ooo" on hole number one?

2. Now try drawing in on hole number 4 and say "oy-u" as you are drawing in. Can you hear the shift?

3. Now try either "wee-ooo" or "oy-u" on the 2nd hole draw, 3rd hole draw, as well as the 4th, 5th, and 6th hole draw notes. Every hole responds a little differently to the air pressure. In time you will begin to feel the subtle differences between these bent notes.

Another technique used for learning how to bend is what I call the "cheater technique." As you are drawing in on the 1st hole, increase your air flow gradually while also tilting the harmonica either up or down (pick one direction only). This will cause the air to affect the reeds in the same way that is needed to bend using the previously mentioned technique.

Once you can hear the change of pitch, it is time to learn how to control this technique. Since all notes on the harmonica respond differently to bending, you'll need to know which ones to focus on.

- In the lower register (holes 1 through 6), note bending is achieved by drawing. The 3rd hole is the most easily bent.

- The middle and upper registers (holes 6 through 10) are bent by blowing. The higher you go the more air pressure is required for bending. This is for your information as we will not be using blow bends in this book.

Bending Tips

With respect to the shape of your mouth, we pucker our lips, drop our tongue down, and increase the air pressure, causing the pitch to alter. In order to bend properly, greater air pressure is needed. However, too much air pressure will over-blow the reeds or "choke" the harp. You will simply need to practice to get the feel of how much pressure is needed for each note.

Track 41

Here's a good exercise for practicing your low register half bends.

1↘ Hold   2↘ Hold   3↘ Hold

4↘ Hold   5↘ Hold   6↘ Hold

Track 42

Or, we can mix it up a little.

2↘   1↘   1↘   2↘   4↘   3↘

3↘   4↘   6↘   5↘   5↘   6↘

2↘ Hold

Excellent! Now, take a rest from the bends and try the G blues scale bend-free.

First going up...

$$2\downarrow \quad 3\downarrow \quad 4\uparrow \quad 4\downarrow \quad 5\downarrow \quad 6\uparrow$$

Now going down...

$$6\uparrow \quad 5\downarrow \quad 4\downarrow \quad 4\uparrow \quad 3\downarrow \quad 2\downarrow$$

Great!

More on Bending

When bent notes are written out for harmonica, the following symbols are used:

↘ = Half Bend

↘ = Whole Bend

Practice Bending:

Try the half bend with the 2nd hole draw.

2↘ Hold | 2↘ Hold | 2↘ Hold | 2↘ Hold

Good! Now, let's try the 3rd hole.

3↘ Hold | 3↘ Hold

Okay. Let's try the whole bend a few times.

3↘ Hold | 3↘ Hold

Back to the 3rd hole draw.

3↓ Hold

Now, try the 3rd hole draw half bend.

3↘ Hold

Good! Now, holes 4 and 6.

4↘ Hold | 6↘ Hold | 4↘ Hold | 6↘ Hold

Grace Note Bends

Another common way to play bends on the harmonica is with a *grace note bend*. This is a little easier to accomplish than a regular bend because all you need to do is *pre-bend* the note and then very quickly release it to the regular diatonic note, instead of holding the bend. The next song features this technique. Listen to the CD to get a feel for grace note bends.

Okay. Let's try a simple fiddle tune in second position with a 3rd hole grace note bend. A grace note bend starts on a pre-bent note and then immediately releases to the target note. You'll understand when I demonstrate. This is your first attempt at incorporating any kind of bend into a song. So, take your time and listen to the CD a few times.

Track 46

Shortenin' Bread #1

► If you can't quite get the 3rd hole grace note bend, use your right hand to shape the "wah-wah" sound as it comes out.

Great! Now, go back and try to play it both with music and by memory (by ear!). Once you can do this, try playing it a little faster. Remember to tap your toe in time.

Playing Octaves

Track 47

Before we can play the next piece we need to learn a new technique called *playing octaves*. An octave is the distance or interval (eight notes) between two notes that have the same name. Here's how to play octaves on the harmonica:

- Find the 1st and 4th hole.

- Now, take the tip of your tongue and cover up holes 2 and 3 while blowing into the 1st and 4th holes.

Can you hear how full it sounds? Using the same technique of covering holes 2 and 3, try drawing in on holes 1 and 4. Can you hear two D notes?

Next, take the tip of your tongue and cover up holes 3 and 4 while blowing into holes 2 and 5 simultaneously. You'll hear two E notes. Now, take the tip of your tongue and cover up holes 4 and 5 while blowing into holes 3 and 6. You will get two G notes to ring out together.

This version of "Shortenin' Bread" will teach you to play cross-harp style along with single notes, octaves, and grace note bends… a real show stopper!

Track 48

Shortenin' Bread #2

This wonderful little arrangement shows how to accompany a fiddle tune melody with bends.

Boil Them Cabbage Down #3

This arrangement will teach you how to play with and backup a fiddle tune in cross-harp style by utilizing single notes, bends, and chords.

Boil Them Cabbage Down #3 (Backup)

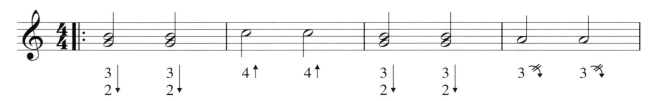

Play 3 times

The Next Level

Track 51

Building Speed

Once you have mastered playing single notes, tremolo, simple bends, and the art of playing your harmonica rhythmically, you should begin to focus on your speed. Playing fast requires confidence and knowledge of the first and second positions:

First Position

4↑ 4↓ 5↑ 5↓ 6↑ 6↓ 7↓ 7↑

Second Position (without bends)

2↓ 3↓ 4↑ 4↓ 5↓ 6↑

American fiddle tunes make great exercises for building speed as they are very scale-like in nature and they sound great. These sorts of melodies are meant to be played fast enough for people to square dance to them. Start off slowly and gradually build up speed until you can play along with the CD, or your friends start to swing one another do-si-do!

Track 52

Old Joe Clark

Here is an additional exercise for building speed.

4↑ 4↓ 5↑ 4↑   4↓ 5↑ 5↓ 4↓   5↑ 5↓ 6↑ 5↑

5↓ 6↑ 6↓ 5↓   6↑ 6↓ 7↓ 6↑   6↓ 7↓ 7↑ 6↓

7↓ 7↑ 8↓ 7↓   7↑

Track 53

Once again, here's another tune that offers us a chance to practice our 3rd hole bends. If you can get these whole bends down, the rest should be easy.

Simple Boogie in G (Cross Harp in G)

► Remember to listen to the warm-up track on the CD.

2↓ 3↓ 4↓ 5↑   5↓ 5↑ 4↓ 3↓   2↓ 3↓ 4↓ 5↑   5↓ 5↑ 4↓ 3↓

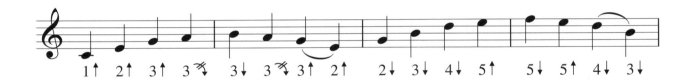

1↑ 2↑ 3↑ 3↘ 3↓ 3↘ 3↑ 2↑   2↓ 3↓ 4↓ 5↑   5↓ 5↑ 4↓ 3↓

1↓ 4↓ 4↑ 4↓   1↑ 4↑ 3↓ 3↑ 2↑   2↓   1↓ 2↑   2↓ 2↑ 1↑ 1↓

Music History

This familiar boogie was inspired by the walking bassline and barrel-house piano players. The boogie is a fun, lively ploy for making the harmonica swing. Recommended listening: any recording by Big Walter Horton, Carl Perkins, Chuck Berry, Leadbelly, and Sonny Boy Williamson.

The Classic Blues Riff

Here is one of the all-time greatest harmonica riffs ever recorded by Little Walter when he was backing up Muddy Waters. It is immediately recognizable and most folks will say, "I've heard that before." The key to playing this catchy little phrase correctly is timing.

Here's how it works:

1. Play the 2nd hole draw (2↓) and hold it.

2. Now play the 4th hole blow (4↑) and hold it.

3. Lastly, play the 3rd and 2nd hole draw notes one right after the other (3↓ 2↓).

When you put all of this together, you get this catchy little phrase:

Play 2↓ hold, 4↑ hold, then play these two fast: 3↓ 2↓.

Try it again. This time add a little rhythm with some chords. Say the words (no voice) as indicated over the chords, short and strong "sh," "k," and "d" sounds.

				shuck	dah	shuck	dah
2↓	4↑	3↓	2↓	3 2 1↓	3 2 1↓	3 2 1↓	3 2 1↓

A variation on this riff can be played like this:

					shuck	dah	shuck	dah
4↓	5↓	4↓	5↓	6↑	3 2 1↓	3 2 1↓	3 2 1↓	3 2 1↓

Third Position (Dorian Mode)

As mentioned earlier, playing the harmonica in third position allows us to play in a minor key. With the key of C harmonica, we can play in D minor. Well, not quite D minor (because in D minor the B is flatted), but D–E–F–G–A–B–C–D, which is actually the *Dorian* mode, does give that minor feeling.

The next two songs, "Scarborough Fair" and "Poor Wayfaring Stranger," are played in third position or Dorian mode.

Try this exercise first and repeat it a few times. It will help you get more comfortable with this key.

4↓ 5↑ 6↑ 5↓ 6↓ 6↑ 5↓ 4↓

Now play the scale a few times.

4↓ 5↑ 5↓ 6↑ 6↓ 7↓ 7↑ 8↓

Great, now let's play an old familiar melody most commonly associated with Simon & Garfunkel. Note that the guitar plays a four-measure introduction before the harmonica part begins in the following two songs.

Track 55

► This song sounds great with tremolo.

Scarborough Fair

4↓ 4↓ 6↓ 6↓ 5↑ 5↓ 5↑ 4↓   6↓ 7↑ 8↓ 7↑

6↓ 7↓ 6↑ 6↓   6↓ 8↓ 8↓ 7↑ 6↓ 6↓ 6↑ 5↓ 5↑ 4↑

4↓ 4↓ 6↓ 6↑ 5↓ 5↑ 4↓ 4↑ 4↓

This very old, sacred melody is loved the world over. This song is great practice for playing in minor keys, but don't forget to employ the use of tremolo.

Track 56

Poor Wayfaring Stranger

Fourth Position (A Minor)

With the key of C harmonica we can also play in the key of A minor or fourth position by beginning with a 6th hole draw and continuing to play the A minor scale as follows:

A	B	C	D	E	F	G	A
6↓	7↓	7↑	8↓	8↑	9↓	9↑	10↓

Notice that the minor keys A and D lend a more mournful sound to the music. As you continue to improve, consider trying some other classics like "Summertime," "Blue Skies," "House of the Rising Sun," and "Shady Grove."

Here's a lovely melody that is an excellent exercise for reading eighth notes, playing in the higher register, and using tremolo. Also in this song I've added some *slides*. A slide (/) is performed by starting on a lower part of the harmonica and "sliding" up to the desired note or chord. You'll understand as soon as you have listened to the CD, in fact, you've already heard some slides used earlier on the CD. See if you can hear which songs include slides. In the key of A minor or fourth position, here is "Hatikvah (With Hope)." It is my hope that this book has helped you along to many years of pleasure playing the harmonica!

Track 57

Hatikvah (With Hope)

Lesson 12 | Harmonica Heroes

Over the last 100 years there have been many harmonica legends. Below is a list of the most important players across the continuum of many styles. It is my sincere hope that the student will seek out the recordings of these players and devote themselves to listening and absorbing the licks, songs, and phrases of the great masters.

Deford Bailey is from Davidson County, Tennessee. This great player from the early 1920s and 30s was the first African American on the Grand Ole Opry. He performed breath-taking, show-stopping renditions of train pieces, fox chases, sacred numbers, and talking harmonica pieces.

Sonny Terry is best known for his highly rhythmic style of playing both solo and with Brownie McGhee. If you want to hear just how percussive a harp can sound, listening to Sonny Terry is a must.

Sonny Boy Williamson (Rice Miller) inspired a generation of both American and British invasion artists with his lyrical, down-home phrasing, and electric Chicago blues. His tone was crisp and clear, and his chops were very lyrical

Little Walter is said to be the first to really push the limits of the harmonica through ampli-fication and incorporating jazz-like horn lines into his playing. His big hit was the classic harmonica solo, "Juke." He performed both under his own name and as a side man for Muddy Waters.

Big Walter, like Little Walter, was a Chicago-based performer and recording artist whose big, fat tone was as rich and shaky as anyone could want. He recorded both under his own name and as a side man.

Charlie McCoy is the quintessential country-western harmonica player. Both inventive and rooted, Charlie's playing graces hundreds of albums in country, rock, and folk.

Mike Stevens stands today as one of the greatest living proponents of the bluegrass style, playing fiddle tunes, train pieces, and bluegrass standards.

Howard Levy is the single greatest living harmonica player on the planet!

PLAY TODAY® SERIES

THE ULTIMATE SELF-TEACHING SERIES!

How many times have you said: "I wish I would've learned to play guitar… piano… saxophone…" Well, it's time to do something about it. The revolutionary *Play Today!* Series from Hal Leonard will get you doing what you've always wanted to do: make music. Best of all, with these book/CD packs you can listen and learn at your own pace, in the comfort of your own home!

This method can be used by students who want to teach themselves or by teachers for private or group instruction. It is a complete guide to the basics, designed to offer quality instruction in the book and on the CD, terrific songs, and a professional-quality CD with tons of full-demo tracks and audio instruction. Each book includes over 70 great songs and examples!

Play Guitar Today! `DVD` `CD` `INCLUDES TAB`
00696100 Level 1 Book/CD Pack....................................$9.95
00696101 Level 2 Book/CD Pack....................................$9.95
00320353 DVD $14.95
00696102 Songbook Book/CD Pack..............................$12.95
00699544 Beginner's Pack – Level 1 Book/CD & DVD $19.95
00842055 Play Today Plus Book/CD Pack.....................$14.95

Play Bass Today! `DVD` `CD` `INCLUDES TAB`
00842020 Level 1 Book/CD Pack....................................$9.95
00842036 Level 2 Book/CD Pack....................................$9.95
00320356 DVD $14.95
00842037 Songbook Book/CD Pack..............................$12.95
00699552 Beginner's Pack – Level 1 Book/CD & DVD $19.95
00698997 Play Today Plus Book/CD Pack.....................$14.95

Play Drums Today! `DVD` `CD`
00842021 Level 1 Book/CD Pack....................................$9.95
00842038 Level 2 Book/CD Pack....................................$9.95
00320355 DVD $14.95
00842039 Songbook Book/CD Pack..............................$12.95
00699551 Beginner's Pack – Level 1 Book/CD & DVD $19.95
00699001 Play Today Plus Book/CD Pack.....................$14.95

Play Piano Today! `DVD` `CD`
00842019 Level 1 Book/CD Pack....................................$9.95
00842040 Level 2 Book/CD Pack....................................$9.95
00320354 DVD $14.95
00842041 Songbook Book/CD Pack..............................$12.95
00699545 Beginner's Pack – Level 1 Book/CD & DVD $19.95
00699044 Play Today Plus Book/CD Pack.....................$14.95

Sing Today! `CD`
00699761 Level 1 Book/CD Pack....................................$9.95

Play Ukulele Today! `CD`
00699638 Level 1 Book/CD Pack....................................$9.95
00699655 Play Today Plus Book/CD Pack.......................$9.95

Play Alto Sax Today! `DVD` `CD`
00842049 Level 1 Book/CD Pack....................................$9.95
00842050 Level 2 Book/CD Pack....................................$9.95
00320359 DVD $14.95
00842051 Songbook Book/CD Pack..............................$12.95
00699555 Beginner's Pack – Level 1 Book/CD & DVD $19.95
00699492 Play Today Plus Book/CD Pack.....................$14.95

Play Flute Today! `DVD` `CD`
00842043 Level 1 Book/CD Pack....................................$9.95
00842044 Level 2 Book/CD Pack....................................$9.95
00320360 DVD $14.95
00842045 Songbook Book/CD Pack..............................$12.95
00699553 Beginner's Pack – Level 1 Book/CD & DVD $19.95
00699489 Play Today Plus Book/CD Pack.....................$14.95

Play Clarinet Today! `DVD` `CD`
00842046 Level 1 Book/CD Pack....................................$9.95
00842047 Level 2 Book/CD Pack....................................$9.95
00320358 DVD $14.95
00842048 Songbook Book/CD Pack..............................$12.95
00699554 Beginner's Pack – Level 1 Book/CD & DVD $19.95
00699490 Play Today Plus Book/CD Pack.....................$14.95

Play Trumpet Today! `DVD` `CD`
00842052 Level 1 Book/CD Pack....................................$9.95
00842053 Level 2 Book/CD Pack....................................$9.95
00320357 DVD $14.95
00842054 Songbook Book/CD Pack..............................$12.95
00699556 Beginner's Pack – Level 1 Book/CD & DVD $19.95
00699491 Play Today Plus Book/CD Pack.....................$14.95

Play Trombone Today! `DVD` `CD`
00699917 Level 1 Book/CD Pack....................................$9.95
00320508 DVD..$14.95

Play Violin Today! `CD`
00699748 Level 1 Book/CD Pack....................................$9.95

Play Recorder Today! `CD`
00700919 Level 1 Book/CD Pack....................................$7.95

FOR MORE INFORMATION, SEE YOUR LOCAL MUSIC DEALER, OR WRITE TO:

HAL•LEONARD® CORPORATION

7777 W. BLUEMOUND RD. P.O. BOX 13819 MILWAUKEE, WI 53213

Visit us online at **www.halleonard.com**

Prices, contents and availability subject to change without notice.

0809